DIGGING INTO HISTORY

SOLVING THE MYSTERIES OF
POMPEII

Charlie Samuel

FRANKLIN WATTS
LONDON•SYDNEY

This edition first published in 2010
by Franklin Watts
338 Euston Road
London NW1 3BH

Franklin Watts Australia
Level 17/207 Kent Street
Sydney, NSW 2000

A CIP catalogue record for this book is available
from the British Library.

ISBN: 978 0 7496 9495 1

Dewey number: 937.7

Printed in Malaysia

Franklin Watts is a division of
Hachette Children's Books,
an Hachette UK company.
www.hachette.co.uk

Note to parents and teachers concerning
websites: In the book every effort has been
made by the Publishers to ensure that
websites are suitable for children, that they
are of the highest educational value, and that
they contain no inappropriate or offensive
material. However, because of the nature of
the Internet, it is impossible to guarantee that
the contents of these sites will not be altered.
We advise that Internet access is supervised
by a responsible adult.

For The Brown Reference Group Ltd
Designer: Dave Allen
Picture Researcher: Clare Newman
Managing Editor: Tim Cooke
Indexer: Kay Ollerenshaw
Editorial Director: Lindsey Lowe

Picture Credits
The photographs in this book are used by
permission and through the courtesy of:

Front Cover: John Lumb/Shutterstock

Corbis: Bettmann 11, Jonathan Blair 15, Christie's
Images 10, Araldo De Luca 24, Ciro Fusco/epa
13b, Richard T. Nowitz 23, Vittoviano Rastelli
26–27, Roger Ressmeyer 4–5, Sean Sexton
Collection 13t, Vince Streano 28; DeAgostini
Picture Library: 19b, 22; MEPL: 5; NGIC: Jonathan
Blair 14b, O. Louis Mazzatenta 6, Richard Nowitz
14t; Procedural Inc: Pascall Mueller, Simon Haegler
& Andreas Ulmer 18; Shutterstock: Danilo Ascione
7b, 16–17, 25, Pavel K 21, Vladimir Korostyshevskiy
8, John Lumb 12, Pierdelune 7t, Thomas Pozzo Di
Borgo 9; Werner Forman Archive: 19t, 20, 29.

Contents

WHO FOUND THE BURIED CITIES?

TWO ROMAN CITIES WERE BURIED FOR CENTURIES. BUT WHEN THEY WERE FIRST DISCOVERED, FEW PEOPLE WERE INTERESTED IN UNCOVERING THEM.

In the early 1700s, workers began digging a well near the foot of Vesuvius, a volcano that rises above the Bay of Naples in southern Italy. They found statues of women dressed in the style of ancient Romans. A few decades later, in 1734, the area around Naples came under the control of a new king, Charles VII. He sent troops to the site to look for more old objects. Many people collected pieces of Roman art. The soldiers found more statues. They also

found something that seemed worthless but was far more valuable to historians. It was a piece of stone carved with the Latin for 'the theatre of Herculaneum'.

Roman writers recorded the destruction of the city of Herculaneum by an eruption of Vesuvius in the first century CE. The city had been buried for more than 1,500 years.

A SECOND CITY

The ancient writers said that another city was also destroyed – Pompeii. In 1748 Charles's soldiers began digging at a hillside some 9.5 kilometres (6 miles)

southeast of Vesuvius, where people had found old **artefacts**. The soldiers soon uncovered walls, carvings and skeletons. Was this Pompeii? No one cared, as long as they found treasure. But fifteen years later a name carved on a wall showed that this was indeed the lost city of Pompeii.

SAVE THE CITIES

The treasure hunt went on for 200 years. Workers even used gunpowder

BELOW: *The excavated ruins of Pompeii stand amid the modern landscape. Vesuvius, the volcano that destroyed the city in 79 CE, rises in the background.*

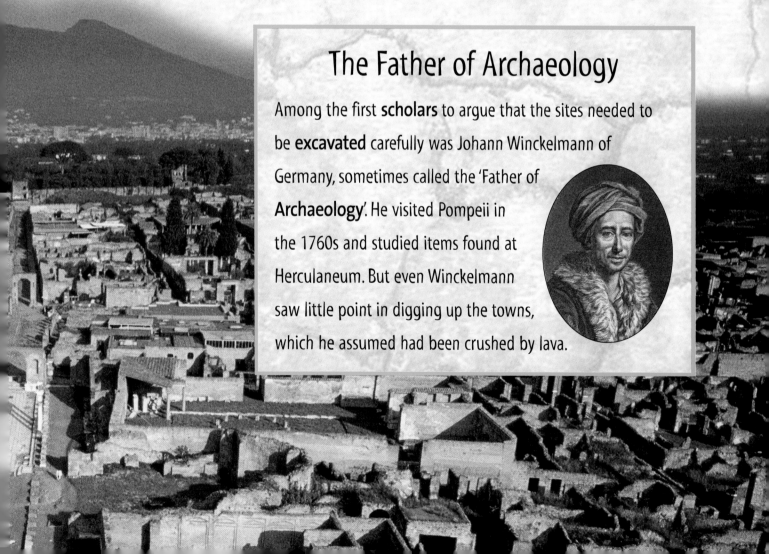

The Father of Archaeology

Among the first **scholars** to argue that the sites needed to be **excavated** carefully was Johann Winckelmann of Germany, sometimes called the 'Father of Archaeology'. He visited Pompeii in the 1760s and studied items found at Herculaneum. But even Winckelmann saw little point in digging up the towns, which he assumed had been crushed by lava.

Working to a System

Early excavations destroyed many ruins and artefacts at Pompeii and Herculaneum. Today, archaeologists are much more careful because anything might be useful for understanding the past. Archaeologists work like detectives at a crime scene. They take photographs and make drawings to show not just what they find, but where they find it. Archaeologists know they can learn as much from a brick wall as they can from a coin or statue. When they have finished excavating and have removed artefacts for analysis, they will still have a record of what the site looked like when it was first uncovered.

?

DID YOU KNOW

Buried objects turn up in layers in the soil called **strata**, which help reveal their age: the lower the strata, the older the objects.

BELOW: *An expert pieces together a broken mosaic from Pompeii.*

to blast holes. However, some people began to argue that the cities themselves were as valuable as the statues. They could show us how the Romans lived.

A NEW APPROACH

In 1860, Italian archaeologist Giuseppe Fiorelli took charge at Pompeii. He wanted to uncover the whole city. His workers systematically cleared buildings, blocks and neighbourhoods. They left artefacts in their original positions, where experts could study them. Slowly, Pompeii began to come back to life.

ABOVE: *Experts have reconstructed some of the wooden roofs and awnings on this street in Herculaneum.*

A Common Language

Sometimes archaeologists studying ancient civilisations find writing in languages they do not know how to read. Experts studying Herculaneum and Pompeii are lucky. They understand the language the people spoke. Latin was used throughout the Roman **Empire**. It is not spoken anymore, but it is the basis of languages such as Italian and Spanish. That makes it quite easy to learn. Experts can read most of the written records of the ancient Romans. At Pompeii they can read **inscriptions** on objects,

BELOW: *According to this inscription, a man named Numerius Popidius Celsinus rebuilt the Temple of Isis in Pompeii after an earthquake destroyed the great building in 62 CE.*

letters and other documents, as well as messages scratched on the walls.

How Do You Lose a City?

The history of archaeology is full of stories of the discoveries of famous 'lost' cities. Some have been buried, either accidentally like Pompeii and Herculaneum, or deliberately. When the Spanish conquered the Aztec Empire in the sixteenth century, they deliberately built a new city on top of the Aztec capital, Tenochtitlán. Some cities are abandoned, like Troy, which was found beneath a mound of earth in present-day Turkey. Others are slowly forgotten, like the Incan city of

? DID YOU KNOW

Local people forgot that Angkor in Cambodia had been built by their ancestors. They told Europeans it was built by gods.

FAMOUS LOST CITIES

- Troy, Turkey
- Angkor, Cambodia (below)
- Machu Picchu, Peru
- Mohenjo Daro, Pakistan

ABOVE: *Pyramids peek from the rain forest at Tikal in Guatemala. Once the Mayan city was abandoned, the forest soon covered it up.*

Machu Picchu in the mountains of Peru or Angkor, built by the Khmer in the forests of Cambodia. But are these cities ever truly lost? Although their locations may not be known to archaeologists, local people usually know that they are there. After all, it's difficult to hide something as big as a city! When the American Hiram Bingham 'discovered' Machu Picchu in 1911, for example, local farmers were living among the ruins.

One clue to the location of old cities comes from place names. Local people called the site of Pompeii La Civita,

LEFT: *When experts found the ruins of Angkor in Cambodia in the nineteenth century, local people believed the city had been built by gods.*

from the Latin word *civitas*, or 'city'. The site of Troy was called Hissarlik, or 'the place of the palace'. In what is now Pakistan, archaeologists explored a place named Mohenjo Daro – 'mound of the dead'. Guess what they found? The burial ground of a huge ancient city.

WHEN LOST ISN'T LOST AT ALL

It turns out that virtually none of the lost cities has ever really disappeared. It would probably come as a surprise to the people who live near them that they were ever considered lost in the first place.

WHAT HAPPENED ON THE DAY OF DISASTER?

ON 24 AUGUST, 79 CE, PEOPLE LIVING NEAR THE FOOT OF VESUVIUS WITNESSED THE TERRIFYING POWER OF A VOLCANO.

Experts know a lot about the day that Pompeii and Herculaneum were destroyed. One clue comes from bodies buried in ash from the volcano. Hundreds of bodies have been found at Pompeii. They include whole families, a maid carrying a bag of possessions and even pets.

The bodies capture part of the terrifying events of 24 August, 79 CE.

ABOVE: *Plaster casts show where a family from Pompeii tried to shelter beneath a wall – but it could not save them from the falling ash.*

A TERRIFYING DAY

For days, the ground around Vesuvius had been shaking. The volcano had not erupted for 1,000 years, but the area had experienced earthquakes. Some people got frightened and moved away.

Early on 24 August, smoke and ash began to rise from Vesuvius. Then, at 1 PM, the volcano **erupted**. It shot molten rock and debris 27 kilometres (17 miles) into the sky.

People panicked as rocks and a stone called **pumice** rained down on Pompeii. Some people were killed by falling rocks or roofs that collapsed under the growing weight of the pumice.

LEFT: *This painting by Charles François Lacroix shows a 1777 eruption of Vesuvius. The volcano has erupted many times in the last five hundred years.*

Preserving the Remains

In the 1860s, Giuseppe Fiorelli noticed that workers excavating Pompeii sometimes came across what seemed to be empty spaces in the ground. Fiorelli suddenly guessed that the spaces might once have held the bodies of people who died fleeing the city. While the ash hardened into rock over the centuries, the people's bodies would have decayed. But they would leave a hole in the stone that was the same shape as the person.

When a worker found another empty space in the stone, Fiorelli made a small hole and poured liquid plaster in to fill up the space inside. When the plaster set and the workers cleared the hardened **lava** away, the **plaster cast** revealed one of the terrified citizens of Pompeii, who had been buried in the ash. Fiorelli's technique is still used to reveal the bodies of the dead, only today plastics are used instead of plaster.

BELOW: *Only the skull was still in place on this body – the rest was cast in plaster.*

Over the next few hours, most people left the city. About two thousand stayed behind. Perhaps they were worried about leaving their homes or businesses. But by late afternoon, pumice blocked the streets. People were stuck. They choked on the dust or were buried by falling ash.

A WAVE OF DEATH

On the western side of the volcano, the wind had blown the cloud of smoke and ash away from Herculaneum. The town seemed safe. But at about 1 AM, twelve

hours after the eruption, a stream of boiling hot gas, rock and pumice shot out of the side of the volcano – straight at the town. Experts can piece together what happened by studying more recent eruptions. A wave of gas and ash swept down the hillside at a speed of up to 160 kilometres (100 miles) per hour. It would have taken just 4 minutes to reach Herculaneum. The force of the wave knocked down homes and filled the lungs of every living thing in its way. No one could survive. The ash cloud swept into the sea, where it made the water boil. Soon, a wall of super-hot melted rock, called lava, flowed over Herculaneum, filling it until all trace of the town was buried. Shortly afterwards, another cloud of gas and ash raced down towards Pompeii, killing any survivors left in that city.

ABOVE: *Pets died with their owners. This greyhound was tumbled over by the wave of ash and rock.*

BELOW: *Experts can reconstruct faces by taking precise measurements of skulls. The face on the right is a computer-generated image based on the skull on the left.*

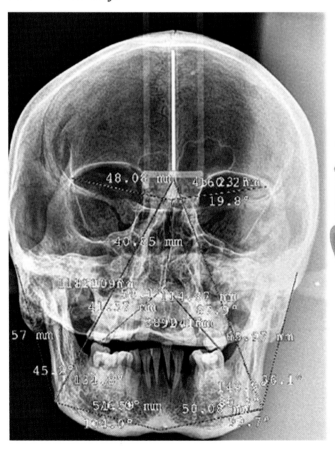

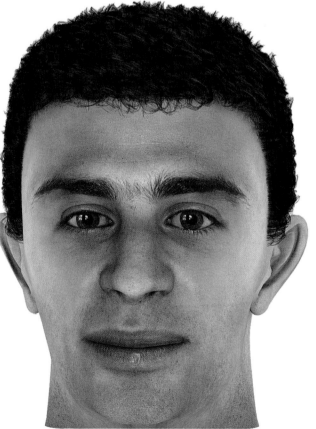

Lessons from Bones

Before 1980, few bodies had been found at Herculaneum. Most experts believed that the residents had fled. Then Italian archaeologists working near what had been the coastline found evidence that not everyone had escaped. There were one hundred and fifty skeletons huddled in archways along the shore. Nearby, on the beach, excavators found a skeleton near a boat. They believe that the man may have been trying to escape by sea. There was also a skeleton with a

ABOVE: *This horse died at Pompeii. The city was full of horses and oxen that pulled carts. When the eruption began, some fleeing citizens abandoned their animals.*

ABOVE: *An archaeologist cleans the skeleton of a man found on the beach at Herculaneum. A sword lies at the man's side, so he may have been a soldier.*

sword by its side. Perhaps it was that of a soldier who had been trying to control the crowd as the volcano's deadly cloud sped towards them.

BONE BONANZA

Roman skeletons are very rare because the Romans cremated, or burned, dead bodies. For archaeologists, skeletons provide a huge amount of information. By measuring the length of the arm and leg bones, experts can tell how tall a

ABOVE: *This is the skeleton of a noblewoman from Herculaneum. She still wears rings on her fingers.*

person was. The bones reveal the person's age when he or she died. Analysis of bones also reveals any diseases that people suffered from or what their main sources of food were. At Herculaneum, the bones revealed that people had absorbed dangerous amounts of lead – a metal the Romans used to store wine.

Respect for the Dead

Archaeologists often clash with people who believe that ancient remains should be left alone. Some groups descended from ancient peoples protest against the excavation of their ancestors' bodies. However, bodies reveal so much that scientists cannot ignore them – but they are careful to treat them with respect.

WHAT WERE THE CITIES LIKE?

ALTHOUGH LITTLE OF HERCULANEUM HAS BEEN EXCAVATED, AT POMPEII EXCAVATIONS REVEAL THE SHAPE OF A ROMAN CITY.

At its height in 117 CE, the Roman Empire stretched from North Africa to northern Europe and from the Atlantic in the west to the borders of present-day Russia in the east. The Romans built cities all over their empire. Cities had houses and palaces, temples for worship, forts and walls for defence, theatres and baths with steam rooms. Straight roads connected cities

and towns and enabled soldiers and goods to move around quickly.

Pompeii is the most complete Roman city ever discovered. The stone and ash sealed it like a time capsule. Since the middle of the nineteenth century, the town has been carefully unearthed. After the work was organised by Fiorelli, archaeologists learned to clear buildings from the top down. That made it easier to preserve the walls of the buildings.

A WEALTHY CITY

Pompeii was a wealthy coastal city of about 20,000 people, surrounded by walls almost 3.2 kilometres (2 miles) around. The city gained its wealth from trade. At its heart stood the **forum**, an open rectangle surrounded by covered galleries, the roofs of which rested on pillars. The forum was a meeting place, and a market was held there. It was also the heart of town government. It contained the **basilica**, a large building that was the centre of trade and legal affairs. About forty statues in the forum celebrated gods or emperors. The forum also held the Temple of Jupiter, the largest of at least ten temples in Pompeii.

A TOUR OF THE TOWN

The forum led onto the main shopping street, the 'Street of Plenty', which was lined with small stores and snack bars. Fountains supplied clean drinking water, which was carried all over the city by underground pipes. The streets were lined with gutters that carried away dirty water. People used stepping stones to cross the street without getting their

LEFT: *The streets of Pompeii were lined by high pavements so pedestrians did not have to walk in the dirty roads. The pavements also kept dust out of the buildings.*

17

Virtual Pompeii

One of the most useful tools for archaeologists trying to get an overview of how Pompeii appeared is to create a virtual reality city. At the University of California, Los Angeles, USA, measurements of the ruins are fed into computers that generate highly accurate three-dimensional maps. The maps give a much clearer idea of the relative size of buildings than can be seen with the naked eye. They also allow experts to see rooms from all angles, to place furniture and to add colours to the walls.

VIRTUAL SITES

Some sites that have been recreated on computer are:
- The Colosseum, Rome
- Tenochtitlán, Mexico
- The Acropolis, Athens

BELOW: *A virtual reality reconstruction shows how part of Pompeii may have looked.*

ABOVE: *This room in the public baths at Pompeii was heated by steam in the hollow walls and floor so that bathers would sweat – which helped clean the skin.*

BELOW: *The tiled atrium, or entrance hall, of this Pompeii home had a pool of water that helped keep it cool.*

feet dirty. Some of the dirt came from animals that pulled cartloads of goods through the streets. Cartwheels had worn ruts 25 centimetres (10 inches) deep in some of the paving stones.

Ancient writers noted that Pompeii was famous for making a strong-tasting fish sauce that was popular throughout the Empire. Herculaneum was also a fishing centre. It was a suburb of a larger settlement called Neapolis, which is now the city of Naples. Experts believe that Herculaneum was more industrial than Pompeii, with a fishing fleet and more workshops.

Preserving Paintings

Pompeii and Herculaneum are among the few places where experts can study Roman paintings. Many walls are decorated with scenes of gardens or still lifes of food. One of the most common colours is red – made from a mineral called cinnabar. Excavators have noticed that the red turns black soon after paintings are uncovered. Using **radiation** technology, they learned that the darkening may be caused when paint reacts with salt in the air from the nearby sea. The Romans had complained about the same darkening – they protected the paint by covering it with a layer of wax.

*RIGHT: This mural is part of a shrine dedicated to the **lares**, or gods of the household. Each home had its own shrine to worship its lares.*

To relax, there were two theatres for watching plays. There was an amphitheatre – large enough to seat the entire population – for staging fights between gladiators. Pompeii had three **bathhouses** where people washed and met their friends. The baths must have been popular. When the town was destroyed, a builder was constructing a fourth. The town also had more than one hundred bars.

Pompeii had a reputation as a coastal resort. On the hills near the city, wealthy families from Rome built luxury **villas**. Some villas had up to fifty rooms.

Inside the city, homes ranged from small one-room apartments to much larger villas that were either built around open courtyards or had large gardens. Experts can even identify the kind of plants that grew in the city. One garden was home to so many types of fragrant plants that modern experts believe it must have belonged to a workshop that produced perfume.

ABOVE: *Some parts of the ancient city have been discovered almost intact.*

CHANGES IN THE CITY

In the 1880s and 1890s, the German archaeologist August Mau studied the building materials and different styles of architecture used at Pompeii. The clues he gathered helped him put together a picture of how the city had developed over the centuries. The earliest buildings around the forum, for example, dated from the 300s BCE.

Mau discovered that a big change took place in Pompeii after 62 CE. In that year, a huge earthquake rocked the city. Many rich families moved away. Their homes became workshops. Often, the workshops belonged to **fullers**, the men who washed clothes. For another seventeen years, the city prospered. But that would all change in August 79 CE.

How Not to Rebuild a Roman Villa

The upper storeys of buildings at Pompeii are often missing. In the late nineteenth century, experts began to reconstruct them with modern materials and techniques. Today, some archaeologists argue that using such materials means that the ruins are no longer authentic. It would be more accurate to leave them as they were, rather than to add details that might be wrong or misleading.

HOW DID THE ROMANS LIVE?

ASH AND STONE TURNED POMPEII AND HERCULANEUM INTO TIME CAPSULES THAT GIVE MODERN ARCHAEOLOGISTS A GLIMPSE OF ROMAN LIFE.

The Romans are one of the ancient peoples we know most about today. There are many written accounts of the Romans, both by the Romans themselves and by their neighbours. But most ancient writers did not think it was important to describe ordinary life.

Pompeii and Herculaneum tell that side of the story. Many of the houses are still just as they were on the day of

disaster. There are cooking pots on stoves, meals on tables, letters waiting to be answered, fruit for sale in the market – even loaves of bread waiting to go into the oven. All this is a reminder of how suddenly the eruption of Vesuvius happened.

PAINT THE TOWN RED

One of the biggest surprises in Pompeii is that the walls of the city were painted with bright

LEFT: The Pompeiian version of a restaurant–bar was the thermopolion, where deep bowls kept food warm.

ABOVE: This bowl of walnuts still stands on the table in Pompeii where it was placed 2,000 years ago. The walnuts have become as hard as stone.

What's for Dinner?

Evidence from Pompeii shows that most citizens ate foods such as lentil stew or goat's cheese, often with bread. Up to thirty bakeries ground flour to make round, flat loaves. Wealthy diners lay on couches and enjoyed a number of dishes, such as beef, goose and fish, all eaten with eggs and olives.

Save Our Scrolls

In 1752, workers excavating a large villa at Herculaneum came across a room stacked with scrolls of **papyrus**, or paper. The room was a library of more than 1,800 records written on papyrus that had been rolled up for storage. But what did the scrolls say? The first efforts to find out were a disaster. Cutting the scrolls open only made the paper break into dust. A new method was tried of unrolling the scrolls gently. It worked — but only slowly. It took four years to unroll only three scrolls. Then, in 2005, scientists at the University of Kentucky, USA, developed a way to use X-rays to see inside the scrolls. The words could be read without unrolling the cylinders. Reading all the scrolls will still take years, but experts are very excited about what they might learn.

ABOVE: *This golden snake was worn by a Pompeiian woman to decorate her forearm.*

colours and murals. The walls were also covered with painted shop signs, messages about elections, rules about dumping rubbish and lots of graffiti.

There are about 6,000 pieces of graffiti on the walls. People scratched Latin words into the stone with sharp needles (the word *graffiti* comes from the Latin word for 'scratch'). One phrase sounds like a modern insult: "From Samius to Cornelius: Go hang yourself!"

PEOPLE OF POMPEII

Since the 1920s, archaeologists have concentrated on finding out about the owners of homes and objects at Pompeii. They have learned people's names from legal documents, from seals that people used to close letters, from graffiti or even from labels on jars of wine. It has been difficult to learn much about the people, or to tell who lived where. But some stories have emerged. A woman named Primigenia, for example, seems to have been a great beauty. Men scratched love messages on the walls near her home.

A FISHY TALE

Another man, Aulus Umbricius Scaurus, was a merchant. He grew rich making and selling fish sauce, which Romans used at most meals. He built himself a large villa. In its entrance was a black-and-white floor mosaic that featured pictures of jars – of fish sauce!

Scaurus's money may have been looked after by a banker, Lucius Caecilius Jucundus. At his home, which was excavated in 1875, workers found a sealed chest holding 154 wax tablets. Scratched in the wax were the records of Lucius's customers. The records may help to identify the owners of other homes in the city.

ABOVE: *Putting together hundreds of identical broken pots is one challenge facing archaeologists at Pompeii.*

Pottery Puzzle

Putting together broken pottery is like doing a jigsaw puzzle. At a site such as Pompeii, where many pots may be smashed together, it is like doing lots of jigsaws that have been jumbled up. Experts must record exactly where the pieces are found to see which may belong to the same pot. Then the work begins of laying out the pieces and trying to fit them together. Some archaeologists scan the pieces into computers and fit them together on screen.

25

WHAT HAPPENS NEXT?

ARCHAEOLOGISTS HAVE LEARNED MUCH FROM POMPEII AND HERCULANEUM. FUTURE GENERATIONS WILL LEARN EVEN MORE.

Today, Pompeii and Herculaneum are among the most investigated archaeological sites anywhere in the world. Teams from universities and institutions in Italy and throughout the world work on different parts of the towns. The sites are good places for archaeology students to learn the skills of excavating ancient remains. One team is concentrating on clearing the

granary at Pompeii, for example, while another focuses on putting back together pieces of broken pottery. More than three-fifths of Pompeii has been excavated, but only a few blocks of Herculaneum. What should happen to the sites now?

TO DIG OR NOT TO DIG?

There is still a lot to learn, but getting to the ruins might be difficult. Much of Herculaneum lies beneath the modern

LEFT: An expert analyses finds on a computer at Pompeii. Future improvements in technology will surely unlock many more secrets from the buried cities.

town of Ercolano. Should the Italian authorities order that new buildings be knocked down to allow experts to excavate more of the ancient town?

Virtually all archaeologists who study the Romans say no – but not because they do not want to disturb the modern town. They do think that the sites should both be fully excavated, just not at the moment. These experts believe that the ruins should be left for future generations of experts to explore. Work today should focus on analysing all the evidence that has been gathered in the last two hundred years.

STRONG FUTURE

Technology is always developing. Future archaeologists will have more powerful tools for analysing any artefacts they find. The evidence still

Pompeii and the Imagination

The fate of Pompeii has gripped artists and writers for centuries. More recently, film directors and TV producers have tried to depict the city's last hours. By the end of the twentieth century, special effects created terrifying scenes based on the scientific study of real volcanoes. But the true fascination of the story still lies in imagining the thoughts of the people trapped as the city was buried in volcanic ash.

Treading on History

About 2.5 million people visit Pompeii every year. This creates huge problems, from building car parks to protecting the ruins. Ancient pavements are being worn away. Moisture from tourists' breath and oil from their skin can soften mortar in walls or fade paint in murals. About sixty buildings were once open to visitors. Today, only sixteen are open in an attempt to avoid damage to their interiors. The Italian government wants visitors to keep coming – it raises a lot of money from entrance fees – but it is also trying to limit the damage they do.

SITES IN DANGER

World archaeological sites being damaged by visitors include:
- Machu Picchu, Peru
- Stonehenge, Britain
- The Roman Forum, Italy
- Angkor, Cambodia
- Mesa Verde, USA.

BELOW: *Pompeii attracts 7,000 visitors every day.*

at Pompeii and Herculaneum should be left where it is so that when it is finally dug up it will provide more information.

UNDER THE VOLCANO

While work goes on at both sites, and tourists come and go, one thing has not changed – Vesuvius looms in the background. The volcano has not erupted for nearly 2,000 years, but that does not mean it is extinct. In 1980, a large earthquake struck the Bay of Naples. It destroyed parts of Pompeii that had been excavated and restored. Some of the town had to be closed to visitors for years while the ruins were made safe again. In the archaeological museum in Naples, objects that survived the 79 CE eruption of Vesuvius were smashed. The earthquake was a reminder that the region is still unstable. The kind of disaster that made the buried cities such a unique archaeological record might one day destroy them again.

A QUIET SCENE

For now, the earth is quiet. The streets of Pompeii and Herculaneum lie still in the Italian sunshine. It often feels as if the ancient citizens are somewhere nearby, carrying on with their daily lives.

BELOW: *The garden wall of a house in Pompeii is painted with an African landscape. Perhaps the owner once lived in a Roman colony in North Africa.*

Further Resources

BOOKS

Corbishley, Mike. *The British Museum Illustrated Encyclopedia of Ancient Rome.* British Museum Press, 2003

Deary, Terry. *The Rotten Romans/The Ruthless Romans. Unlocks the Secrets of Rome's Past* Scholastic Hippo, 2007 and 2003

Hull, Robert. *In Their Own Words: Romans.* Franklin Watts, 2001

James, Simon. *Eyewitness Guide to Ancient Rome.* Dorling Kindersley, 2008

Lawrence, Caroline. Roman Mysteries series, including *The Pirates of Pompeii* and *The Secrets of Vesuvius.* Orion Children's Books, various publication dates

Platt, Richard. *Pompeii Through Time.* Kingfisher, 2007

WEB SITES

The BBC website about ancient Rome.
http://www.bbc.co.uk/schools/romans/

Visit the Pompeii part of the BBC's website about ancient Rome.
http://www.bbc.co.uk/history/ancient/romans/daily_life_gallery.shtml

A detailed BBC website about ancient Rome and the Romans.
http://www.bbc.co.uk/history/ancient/romans/index.shtml

The US Public Broadcasting Service website about ancient Rome.
http://www.pbs.org/empires/romans/

The Discovery Channel's pages about Pompeii.
http://dsc.discovery.com/convergence/pompeii/pompeii.html

Glossary

archaeology: The scientific study of cultures by analysing remains such as artefacts and monuments.

artefact: An object that has been made or changed by humans.

basilica: A large oblong building, often with a projecting semicircular section. Basilicas were used as courts or for public meetings. In later times, the word came to refer to a type of church.

bathhouse: A public building where Romans went to wash and to meet their friends. The baths featured steam rooms and cold water pools.

empire: A large area of land in which different peoples are ruled by an emperor or empress.

erupts: When a volcano explodes.

excavation: A scientific dig to explore an archaeological site.

forum: An open space in a Roman city that served as a marketplace and was the centre of public life.

fuller: A person who washes clothing and cloth.

inscription: A word or phrase carved into a hard surface, such as stone.

lares: Roman gods that protected the house and the family.

lava: The molten rock that flows from a volcano.

papyrus: An early type of paper made from a kind of plant called a reed.

plaster cast: A model made by pouring liquid plaster into a mould and allowing it to harden.

pumice: A very light rock ejected by a volcano; the rock is so light because it is porous, or full of pockets of air.

radiation: Energy moving in the form of waves that can be used to examine the atomic structure of objects.

scholar: An expert who has studied a subject in detail.

strata: Layers of rock and earth in the ground (singular: stratum).

villa: A large home in the country built by a wealthy Roman, often as a farm or a vacation home.

Index